The Precarious Tales of the Broken Hearted

Madison McCoy

BookLeaf Publishing

India | USA | UK

Presentation by *BookLeaf Publishing*

Web: www.bookleafpub.com

E-mail: info@bookleafpub.com

ISBN: 9789357447287

First edition 2022

DEDICATION

For my teacher Shannon South, who inspired
me to write

For my aunt Lynn, who loved with all her heart

And to those I haven fallen in love with,

I will never forget your kindness

ACKNOWLEDGEMENT

Thank you to my friends, the teachers that encouraged me, and my mother, who I hope I've made proud.

Sing O' Solomon

Sing O' Solomon
Sing to me
Sing O' Solomon
Pour your light down on me

There's no sweeter wine than you
Draw me up and let's run
I'll be your forever if you'll have me
We are glorious as the moon
As vivacious as the sun
Just tell me when you're ready
And I'll sing

Rise up, Rise up, Rise up my love
Rise up, Rise up, Rise up my dear
Follow, follow the drums

Tell me, you whom my soul loves
Do you want to marry me
We'll be bound, like vines around old trees
You're a lily among the brambles
Our love is tender and sweet
If you left my heart would be in shambles
At twilight, you'll hear me sing

Rise up, Rise up, Rise up my love
Rise up, Rise up, Rise up my dear
Follow, follow the drums

Sing O' Solomon
Sing to me
Sing O' Solomon
Pour your light down on me

The Madrigal Piece

Lioness, witches, and mages
Each more beautiful than we
The Lovers, The Fool, and The Hanged Man
Take my love my darling

My love's hair reminds me of winter
It glows and shimmers and dances like
snow
My love's eyes are like a ducat
They shine bright like gold

Oh my lover breathed me deeply
And I breathed them out
I'd follow them sweetly in the woods
Little did I know that treachery walked
alongside me

A sorceress bore my love away from me
She vexed me, enchanted them
Violet flower wench tore my soul apart
She bore my heart away from me

Oh my lover, taken by a witch
I will mourn my soul and my heart
Broken by a violet-eyed mage
Oh my lover, oh my lover

Homesick

Late nights, long drives, to the gas station on the
corner of Beltline

Getting lost, being found, holding on to the
memories of a ghost, but I feel fine

I heard you're leaving home, taking off to places
unknown, I'm never gonna let you go

Honeysuckles on the back fence, glass in the
streets from burnt out children afraid of growing
up
Rips in my blue jeans, swimming pools and a
cool breeze, I feel homesick but I never left at all

Crayons, red solo cups, parties that last til
midnight with meaningless friends

Overture, moments occur, snap a picture cause
it's all going fast

Staying up late, a clean slate, new beginning
from a childhood's end

Playing outside, red eyes, sick of crying for love
that never lasts, cause we're all growing up so
fast

I heard you're getting on the train, to different
town with a different name, you're not going
alone

Chalk buildings on the sidewalks painted girls
from years of being misunderstood
Mud on little white shoes, laughing and playing
like we had nothing to lose, I feel homesick but I
never left at all

trick or treat and games of tag, little kids running
through the grass remind me of home
Smoking smarties and chewing bubblegum,
coca-cola dreams were a lotta fun but I guess we
all gotta grow up

All Things Are Left Behind

My lord, My God, let Gabriel find me
The air is thick with the prayers left unsung
The thorns of hell dig into the skin
Fear dissolves into something greater than I
Something that delivers me home
There is a sense of belonging in this pain
Sometimes I have no urge to be free
What is existence without pain?
Without hunger?
Without the sting that I know?
It would not be the same, that much I know
I'll let my darling deliver me back to my
kingdom
He will heal my wounds, tend to my ailments
Absolve me of all my sins
Hear me pray to the angel
As my skin bleeds, my body aches
Though it burns, scars and bruises
I love the justice of it
I love how he tries to save me every time

Say It

Say it
Feel the dew of your skin drip onto mine
Allow me to hold your visage between my
fingers
Wrap my passion 'round him as he says he loves
me
There's something in the way he says it
As I lay beside him, the room still and silent
Body's old and tired from the work of the day
and the restlessness provided by the darkness
If he were to touch me, I could show him what
bliss is
Yet he does not, for he is at rest
But he still speaks, though he has drifted off to
sleep
I hear him say it
But it is the wrong name

When Stars Die

My love for you is like the sun
Everything you do and say makes me come
undone
I flare, I freak, I'm completely unprepared for
anything you say to me
Tender whispers, callused hands that hold my
smooth palms
Just say the word darling and I'll give you all of
me
I'll warm your earth, I'll kiss your skin
I'll be the one thing that helps you live
I'll burn so brightly, you'll never give out

There's a drought with your love
It's maddening, hurtful, but I shimmer anyway
You're the only thing that matters to me
You're in my Goldilocks ring
You're in the perfect place, perfect time, and
perfect space to warm you up
Do you ever thank me? No, but that's okay
I'd do it for you every day

But I'm starting to burn out
And I'm afraid of what that means for me
For you

For us
I feel myself expanding, mind quaking,
heartbreaking, soul racing to find out why
Why don't you show your love for me?
What are words without the actions promised?

I'm starting to burn out
If you stay near me, you'll lose yourself within
me
Help me or leave me, either way, it's your call
You're in my orbit, I can't let you go, you have
to let go
Or you have to come closer
Close enough to feel my skin as it cools

I'm going to die
When I do, Stardust will fly
And it'll make a new star, a new sun
A new love
Maybe it'll be better for you
But it's the last straw for me

War

Time stands still when the war is over
You lay down your weapons
Sharp words, heated phrases, cruel intentions are
all dropped on the battlefield
Everything falls silent when the battle is won
Without breath nor words, the puppet strings are
once again in play
When the wooden hands are up above
Anguished cries are muffled into silent rage

There is no turning back from this fight
In order for one to survive
You must cut the cancer from you while it's still
alive
You have survived enough of these battles, you
prayed tirelessly for the end of the war
A warrior digs their heels into the ground
And stares their enemy down
Time stands still and all is silent
Mercy flits across your mind
But why?
Achilles showed no mercy even when Hector
cried
It's not over until the white flag is raised
With your rage and anguish and tears

This battle was meant to be won by you
You set your white flag on fire
And wait for theirs to be flown

I Hear You

I hear you in the drowning voices
I hear you in the softest moments
I hear you in my mind, soul, and heart
What's done is done, the past has gone
Lover, my ears will remember hearing you
My tongue will remember speaking your name
My eyes will remember every perfect
imperfections on your face
And when you go away, I'll remember you
You will say farewell to me
And within the past, the love, the wisdom, and
the hurt
I hear you

Depression (and the fight against it)

Truth dear, speak it
Hear your heart and know it's true
You do not belong here but I do
I shadow your light
you'll try to bask in it but it will not be there
It belongs to me now
You'll reach for the stars but I will take them
from you
They are not yours
they are mine
You will stay here in this prison I have devised
For I am you
and you are mine

You are not me
You are a cloud covering my night sky
I blow strong winds to let the moons delicate
healing light shine on me
I take my starry skies and place them into the
eyes that the world sees because that's me

I am the stars, the tranquil night
You are a mere figment and soon will be locked
away to never break my spirit or merit again
You will always be with me, that much is true
You will always be here, in my fantastical
starscape
But I lock you up in a place from which you'll
never escape
You are not me, but you are mine
And I will grow and you'll be confined to your
bottle
Because you will never break me, but I will
contain you

Star Child

When the galaxy was new, everything was
unique
Every cloud, planet, and comet was dipped in
beauty, bliss, and a heaven-sent afterglow
And I was their sweetheart, their kinswoman
I was their star child
As a little fawn, I stumbled my way through
black holes and constellations
I remember being so fearless, so free
No God to worship, no form I had to be
But the stardust came together and it had gravity
I am drowning on this terrestrial plane
I was meant to shine
to be weightless in that unending, empty sea
How dare they remove me from my nebulae
without an iota of thought?
My dazzle was stripped from me and they
contaminated my soul
My life, once meant for the never-ending sky, is
now a tragedy
I dare them to chastise me when I decide to
break my mold
As my stardust returns home, I will hear their
mellow voices below wail
But above I hear my name
Star Child, Star Child, Star Child

I Wonder What the Angels Think

Whisper to me my sister
Tell me what lover you wish to seek
For I am St. Raphael
A lover has been found, a lover to keep

Though the Angels, hath not so happy in heaven
for I have committed treason
I declared not that love was a sin, but a savior to
our good graces
My siblings have ostracized me for no reason

When I was but a babe I agreed with what they
told
That mortals lives are fleeting
 their hearts fickle
all lonely little creatures
Skin wrapped around bone
Against my better judgment, I replied with
candor
"Isn't that their mold?"

Ah but one thing they could not see or chose not
to look on
There were many souls that shone brightly on
the earth
And I found that love during my empty flight
through the dawn
"Lord," I had whispered softly, "what have you
sent my way?"

In those halls, those ones made of gold and
marble, my feathered siblings in their pews
I heaved and breathed a sigh and wished to
depart that night
For their eyes were watching god, but no deity
could sway me from watching you

Hero's Journey

People always paint a lovely picture of hero's
They make them more than any mortal being
could ever dream to make themselves
They have no color, only shades of imperialistic
wisdom
To have a soul, is to have color
To have color is to be impassioned
And to be impassioned is to be human
Lord, there is nothing more marvelous than to be
human
So why be a demigod? Why be a Grecian
soldier? Why be an emperor who's kingdom
spread across seas?
Why not be here with me?
I will do what no blessing could
I'll make love to the colorful parts of you
Though you are no hero, you are mine
I will enjoy my soulful, my colorful
My wonderful, wonderful human
For as long as I have time

Cheers To My Childhood Friend

To the sweetest of potions
And the driest of wines
To the lover, the dreamer, and the bridge
between them
Lovingly wrapped into a facade
Ah my darling, my darling
My sister from another timeline
We'll sing the worlds hymn till our throats are
red
Let the earth burn from the gorgeous fire we
built
Blades and blazing, scorch my skin softly
To the lover not quite transfixed as such
To the sweetheart whose soul runs far too deep
into the empty parts of me
Fight for me
Stay with me
Love me
Love me as I love you
And that is all I could ever dream of owning

Orpheus

What fire is in my soul?
The candle of life still burns
Through full of toil and strife, though
effortlessly passing by
For my heart, my lover pays no toll
Pass my golden coin to the ferryman to take me
across the river
There across the water, lain my sweetheart
Resist the urge to touch, to kiss, to hold him
once again
I whisper to my darling, or maybe to myself
"Allow me to curl up to the sound of you
speaking my name"
Yet, he replies not, from the bank where my
lover lain
For my heart, my dear pays no toll
But I paid my coin to the ferryman, he would do
the same as I
I climb out of the wooden boat
He was the fire in my soul
But candles often burn out due to the evils of
men
I sink into the shallow waters of the River Styx
And join my lover once again

Pomegranate Seeds

Touch me softly, pink and roses
I want to make you question your sanity
To feel your breathing
And to have you breathe in me
You are the Apple and I am Eve
Yet you are also the viper that spoke to me
Am I the fallen or falling?
Kiss me like an Angel
Touch me like the Devil
Make my skin burn
But let my heart not hurt
Sweetheart, I am a monster
For years I was locked away
Never give a morsel of love nor a heart that
stayed
You have broken metal darling
Freed the creature of her chains
Look at me dear, look at me
You stand before a demon loose from Satan's
reins
And I am ravenous...ravenous
Hungry

My Drug of Choice

Tequila and broken glass all along the floor
I don't even remember what we were arguing for
She's got time, I have patience
Somehow we ended up here
It's not like how it was before

She grabs the broom and I get the dustpan
We ask for forgiveness then go to bed
I wake up early and touch her hand
And she smiles up at me
And I think we can pull ourselves together again

This is not the girl I remember
She's a firecracker, a raging comet with a temper
Her skin is hot as the sun on a summer's day
But that's okay
Because I still love her anyway

Years have passed and we've had some changes
Put down the bottles and picked up party favors
We spend our days laughing and talking about
our dreams
I wish they could see
You're not the same person too me

She pours the coffee, I crack the eggs
She holds my hair up, I remind her to take her
meds
There's nothing to scrape off the floor
There are no secrets locked away anymore
I wish they'd see, the person who she grew to be

This is not the girl I remember
She's peaceful, a doe in the woods by the water
Her skin is cool like the breeze on an autumn
day
And we're okay
 Because I still love her anyway

A Mother's Wish

Fear not my little one, your future is bright and
clear
I shall protect you through darkness and
drought, til evil is nay more near
My own life I'd lay down to protect your happy
young spirit and locks
 My own soul I'd throw hence to save you from
the dark
My freedom I would give, for you to see the
dawn of a new day
I love you more than life itself and nothing shall
stall it, nay

Fear not my little one for your future is near
If it be true and I am not with you then yond
means my love for you was real

I don't know where this path shall wend and I
cannot lead you, for it is not for me to say
whether it's valorous or evil
Yet I know in my soul that the path you'll
choose will be right
Cause at heart you are the sun coequal in the
darkest of nights

I know not our destiny nor how our story ends
but I do know my love runs deeper than the river
bend
So blessed be my little wanderer, my brave yet
fearful fawn
Never forget your darkest hour will be just
before the dawn

Fear not my little one, you are never alone
You have a world of people who love you and
you are nowhere near grown

Benedick and Beatrice

Something about his eyes charmed me ere I
sought solitude
It was a hard life I lived but I had my honor
A blossom of a rose, no, rather a flower that is
left untouched by man, is what grew in my
secret garden
I prided myself on my sagacity, on my strong
head, and an even stronger heart

However, something has begun to fester in my
soul
Something that started out infinitesimal has
grown to such a size that my body cannot
contain it
Affection, tenderness, and all those softer
sentiments leak out of every pore and bleed out
of every vein

I had a hard heart until it melted into something
that makes me feel at home
What has he done to me?

I went from a thorn bush to a bushel of aster or
bloom of a white carnation
I loved him ere I knew his name

Anxiety (and its notions)

My heart is beating loud
I dig my heels into the ground so I never have to hear it
It's hard to breathe
I'm choking on the air that's escaping me
Thump thump thump
I'm gasping I'm crying I'm praying
Thump thump thump
I'm drowning darling
Please save me I'm begging
My lord my god please save me

Lover, can you hear me?
Soulmate, can you find me?
Brother, do you love me?
I'm running out of time
Running out of breath
Out of hope
Out of life
I love you all, I love you all

Sing for me holy angels,

Flap your feathered wings for me
Tonight I drift away
Thump-thump
It is much easier to feel the anguished release
Thump-thump
Hold me in your arms one last time
Make me feel at home again
Thump
Thum
Thu
Th
T

Open thy Heart

How did I survive before I found you
Without sunshine
Nor rain
Nor passion
Nor vigor
Nor warmth
Nor delicate pain
What is existence but stardust and us?
A sweetening virus that burns our world up
There is nothing without your love
The tender caress of your hands
The decadent intimacy that only we have ever
read in fanciful, old, dark academia
This is what was meant to be
This is what it feels to have the grass lick at your
skin
It's dew soaking into your clothes, cooling your
body, and easing your mind
To have the bugs and the birds and the dirt
welcome you home
To lay motionless in your ripe divinity and press
onto you with adoration and tender-hearted
desires
The scent of sweet Lillies steal you away
Steal you away to your father

We haven't got long to stay here
Yet darling I never want to move
Can we sleep always like this?
The flesh crawling far from and close to God
I can hear the nine choirs singing
Their feathered wings thumping a marching tune
Yet I ignore the sounds, the rhythm, the glory of
His call
Just to lay down in the dirt and abandoned
eiderdown for a few more moments with you
How did I survive without you?
Without peace
Nor sanity
Nor God
I wasn't surviving
I was waiting

The Godlike Power
of a Woman

Bow my head, for I have a deity to pray
Fingers wrapped in sin
Ah but my deity never knew
I kissed the ring closest to you

Speak to me, sing my soul
Push deeper down into the empty parts of me
Angels couldn't wind me up in the way you do
And heaven couldn't provide relief such as the
touch of you

Obsidians for eyes and blood made of rubies
The sanctity of my lover will cure every ailment
of mine
It will mend every imperfection on my body
I bend the will of the world to my darling
I am the deity to he